040822

Knock Knock
JOKES

A Buddy Book
by **Ima Laffin**

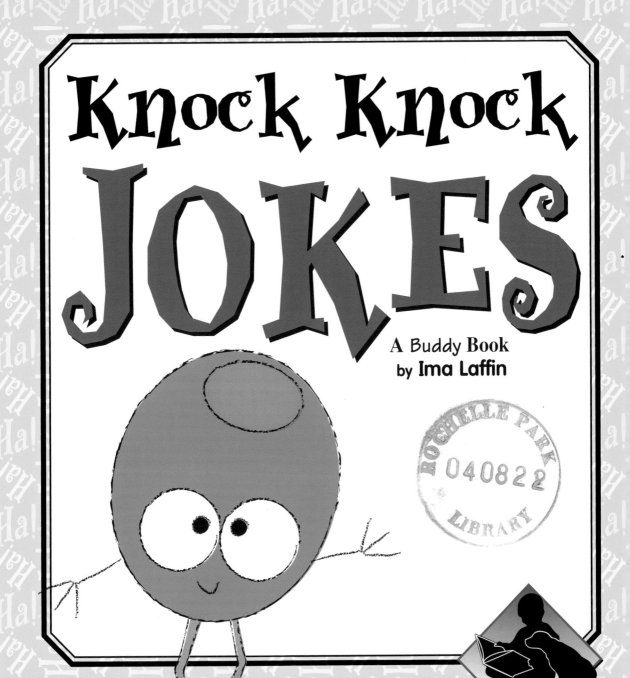

Buddy BOOKS

Jokes

VISIT US AT
www.abdopub.com

Published by ABDO Publishing Company, 4940 Viking Drive, Suite 622, Edina, Minnesota 55435.
Copyright © 2004 by Abdo Consulting Group, Inc. International copyrights reserved in all countries. No
part of this book may be reproduced in any form without written permission from the publisher.

Printed in the United States.

Edited by: Sarah Tieck
Contributing Editors: Matt Ray, Michael P. Goecke
Graphic Design: Deborah Coldiron
Illustrations by: Deborah Coldiron and Maria Hosley

Library of Congress Cataloging-in-Publication Data

Laffin, Ima, 1970-
   Knock-knock jokes / Ima Laffin.
      p. cm. — (Jokes)
   Includes index.
   ISBN 1-59197-622-7
      1. Knock-knock jokes. 2. Wit and humor, Juvenile. [1. Knock-knock jokes. 2. Jokes.] I.
Title. II. Series.

PN6231.K55L36 2004
818'.5402—dc22

                                                            2003069308

Knock knock! Who's there?
Lettuce. Lettuce who?
Lettuce in and I'll tell ya!

Knock knock! Who's there?
Little old lady. Little old lady who?
I didn't know you could yodel!

Knock knock! Who's there?
Want. Want who?
Good! Now try counting to three.

Knock knock! Who's there?
Boo. Boo who?
Don't cry it's only a joke.

Knock knock! Who's there?
Water. Water who?
Water we waiting for?

Knock knock! Who's there?
Repeat. Repeat who?
Who! Who! Who!

Knock knock! Who's there?
Tank. Tank who?
You're welcome!

Knock knock! Who's there?
Amy! Amy who?
Amy fraid I've forgotten!

Knock knock! Who's there?
Peas. Peas who?
Peas to meet you!

Knock knock! Who's there?
Abby! Abby who?
Abby stung me on the nose!

Knock knock! Who's there?
Dot. Dot who?
Dot's for me to know, and you to
find out.

Knock knock! Who's there?
Anita! Anita who?
Anita borrow a pencil!

Knock knock! Who's there?
Philip. Philip who?
Philip my glass please!

Knock knock! Who's there?
Kent. Kent who?
Kent you tell by my voice?

Knock knock! Who's there?
Who. Who who?
You don't who, owls do!

Knock knock! Who's there?
Barb. Barb who?
Barbecue.

Knock knock! Who's there?
Luke. Luke who?
Luke through the keyhole and
find out!

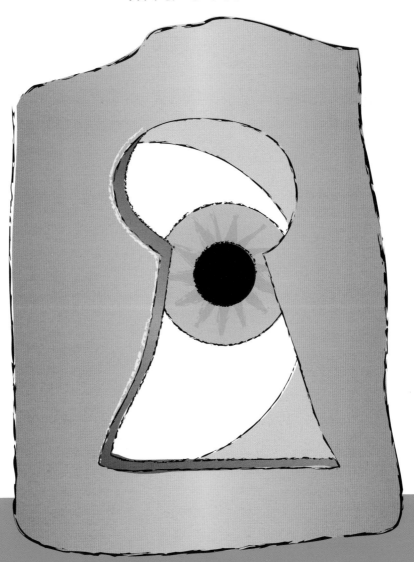

Knock knock! Who's there?
Dishwasher. Dishwasher who?
Dishwasher way I spoke before I
had false teeth!

12

Will you remember me in
a month? Sure.
Will you remember me in
a week? Sure.
Will you remember me in
a day? Sure.
Will you remember me in
an hour? Sure.
Will you remember me in
a minute? Sure.
Will you remember me in
a second? Sure.
Knock knock! Who's there?
You forgot me already!

Knock knock! Who's there?
Amos. Amos who?
A mosquito bit me.

Knock knock! Who's there?
Water. Water who?
Water you doing in my house?

Knock knock! Who's there?
Oink oink. Oink oink who?
Make up your mind if you're going
to be a pig or an owl!

Knock knock! Who's there?
A little girl. A little girl who?
A little girl who can't reach
the doorbell!

Knock knock! Who's there?
Gorilla. Gorilla who?
Gorilla me a sandwich please.

Knock knock! Who's there?
Pig. Pig who?
Pig up your feet or you'll trip!

Knock knock! Who's there?
Isabel. Isabel who?
Isabel necessary on a bicycle?

Knock knock! Who's there?
Doris. Doris who?
Doris open, come on in.

Knock knock! Who's there?
Leaf. Leaf who?
Leaf me alone!

Knock knock! Who's there?
Pudding. Pudding who?
Pudding on your shoes before
your pants is a silly idea!

Knock knock! Who's there?
Tuba. Tuba who?
Tuba toothpaste!

Knock knock! Who's there?
Cargo. Cargo who?
Car go beep beep!

Knock knock! Who's there?
Yah! Yah who?
Did I just hear a cowboy?

Knock knock! Who's there?
Ketchup. Ketchup who?
Ketchup to me and I will
tell you.

Knock knock! Who's there?
Wire. Wire who?
Why are you asking?

Knock knock! Who's there?
Duey. Duey who?
Duey have to keep telling knock
knock jokes?

Knock knock! Who's there?
Police. Police who?
Police stop telling these awful
knock knock jokes!

Knock knock! Who's there?
Candace. Candace who?
Candace be the last knock
knock joke?

Knock knock! Who's there?
Olive. Olive who?
Olive my mom!

Web Sites

Visit ABDO Publishing Company on the World Wide Web. Joke Web sites for children are featured on our Book Links page. These links are monitored and updated to provide the silliest information available.

www.abdopub.com